Vancouver Island

A pictorial tour of Vancouver Island, in the
Province of British Columbia, Canada.
Text by Anne Broadfoot

© Published by Spectrum Enterprises Ltd., Vancouver, British Columbia, Canada

VANCOUVER ISLAND

Vancouver Island is the largest island on the pacific coast of North America, situated on the sunny side of the Strait of Georgia, opposite the mainland of British Columbia.

In 1774, the Spanish Captain Juan Perez, sailing up from old California, scouted the coast now known as British Columbia but did not land or stake any claim. Captain James Cook, the famed British explorer, became the first white man to land in the area when he led two British ships into Nootka Sound on the west coast of the island in 1778. His men traded trinkets to the Indians for sea otter skins and sold the pelts to China merchants at fabulous profits. By 1786, the British had developed a flourishing fur trade at Nootka.

John Meares, an ex-British naval officer and thrifty trader, built a tiny, crude fort at Nootka in 1788 and began a trading tradition that has never been broken. Tall timber for masts and spars were shipped from early Nootka, and today timber in every processed form leaves British Columbia for every continent.

A dispute developed between Britain and the Spanish who claimed the coast because of Perez' earlier voyage. War was avoided by the Nootka Convention of 1790 which awarded both countries equal trading rights and opened the northern Pacific Coast to British settlement.

Captain George Vancouver, an English navigator, arrived in 1792 on a three year surveying voyage and he named many inlets, bays, points and channels.

After a perilous trip through tide-ripped Discovery Passage and the Johnstone Straits, Vancouver proved the territory was indeed an island and it became known as "Quadra and Vancouver's Island". In 1849, the area was established as a British Colony.

This verdant island rises gently from the sea up to a central spine of mountains, topped by the magnificent 7,219 foot Golden Hinde, in Strathcona Provincial Park.

Fir, cedar and hemlock forests cover much of the island and lumbering is the chief industry. Manufacturing allied with the logging industry, mining and fishing are also important to the island's economy.

Vancouver Island is 285 miles long and varies from 40 to 80 miles wide, comprising approximately the same land area as the Netherlands.

Dangerous reefs and islands are strewn along the west coast and many winding deep inlets offer shelter to water craft and add interest to coastal touring. The eastern coast area is less rugged and is home to 95 per cent of the 290,835 inhabitants.

The largest city and provincial capital is Victoria, situated on the southern tip of Vancouver Island.

The warm Japanese current assures a mild year-round climate to the southern portion which averages only 26 inches of precipitation annually. By contrast, the northern and western mountainous regions have rather severe winters. The western coast is buffeted by fierce Pacific gales during the fall and winter.

Last year over 2,000,000 tourists visited Vancouver Island in half a million cars for an average stay of four and one half days, proof that the traveller is well aware of the warm welcome awaiting visitors to Vancouver Island.

Follow the birds . . .

On the marine highway to Vancouver Island.

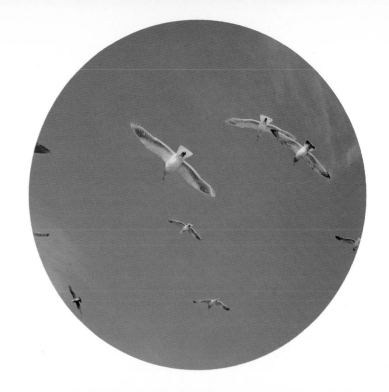

. . . the siren call heeded by those who take the marine highway to Vancouver Island aboard B.C. Government ferries, the world's largest and most modern ferry fleet. The service was inaugurated in 1960, and the ever growing fleet now numbers nineteen snow white vessels with distinctive blue markings on their massive bows.

A traveller is given the option of taking his car aboard, taking a bus from a mid-city depot, or leaving the car in a spacious car park at the ferry slip. Once aboard, able tourist counsellors advise visitors on excursions and activities.

Restful lounges, coffee shops on smaller ferries and full restaurant facilities on the larger ones, plus special innovations such as elevators for invalids on newer vessels, are designed for passengers' comfort.

True to the slogan, ever watchful white gulls trace graceful patterns in the pacific breezes, leading the ferry toward the shores of the Island in an exciting overture to the holiday pleasure ahead.

Adjacent to the new City Hall in mid-town Victoria
is Centennial Fountain, surrounded by this pleasant plaza,
and near a classic Japanese Garden.

VICTORIA

Victoria, the island's largest city and seat of the provincial legislature, is situated on the Saanich peninsula at the southern tip of Vancouver Island.

The Hudson's Bay Company established Fort Victoria in 1843 under Chief Factor James Douglas, who became governor of the colony of Vancouver Island in 1851. The British united the colony of Vancouver Island and the mainland colony of British Columbia in 1866, and in 1868 Victoria was chosen the capital of the merged colony. In 1871, British Columbia became a province of the young Dominion of Canada.

Through the years, Victoria progressed from trading fort to twentieth century city, and today, surrounding an obelisk to Sir James Douglas, there stands a beautiful "Garden City," home of 55,000 people.

Long known as the "retirement capital of Canada," people as well as birds from colder regions of the continent migrate to its temperate climate. Although the birds move on in the spring, many people have remained to settle in and around the city.

Still a favorite retirement spot, Victoria's image is changing. The quaint Victorian atmosphere found in architecture, shops and gardens – long supported by the well known figure of the tweedy, pipe smoking Victorian elder – mixes readily with the boisterous beat of the sixties. Once said to "roll its sidewalks up at nine p.m.", Victoria's young and vibrant generation lays them down again for access to Big Bad John's and other bouncing night spots.

The dignified stone facade of the Empress Hotel, where elegance reigns supreme, looks across the harbor to "go-go" establishments where the mood is definitely casual. Victorians are proud of their little bit of Elizabethan England in Chaucer Lane, and the tea hour still arrives at five, but there is marked civic pride too in the modern stone and steel of the handsome new city hall and other buildings rising steadily.

A bronze figure of the young Queen Victoria stands forever regal on her pedestal before the Parliament Buildings, a reminder of a golden age and a city's vigorous beginnings.

The waters around Victoria are studded with boats of every size, and boating, fishing and golf are favorite recreations all year round.

Air and ferry links between the American and British Columbia mainlands give residents excellent communications with all major cities on the continent, yet allow them to retain a desired measure of isolation on this lovely island.

The invigorating air of Provincial government and the academic tone of a flourishing University also contribute to the enviable image of Victoria – a happy place for old and new.

Red plush carpeting, rich
paneling and dignified columns
surround the symbolic throne
in the Legislative Chamber.

With this memorial citizens
pay homage to those
lost in world wars.

Dominating the view from
Victoria's sea-walled Inner
Harbor, are the grey
stone Parliament buildings.

Government House is the official residence of the Lieutenant Governor, the Queen's representative to the people of British Columbia. These famous Government House gardens are at their most beautiful during the Lieutenant Governor's annual garden fete. The magnificent house, with its imposing pillared gates, is her Majesty's official residence when she visits Victoria.

Craigdarroch Castle was built by coal baron Robert Dunsmuir who mined the rich veins at Nanaimo. He named it Craigdarroch for the Scottish birthplace of Annie Laurie. The castle now houses the school board offices.

This mammoth anchor from a sailing vessel of the past bids welcome to Bastion Square and the dignified entrance of the Maritime Museum. The museum displays a fine collection of artifacts and relics from British Columbia's rich naval history.

Totem poles – silent
sentinels of an earlier
culture in British
Columbia, stand in
Thunderbird Park
along with other
creations of the
Coast Indians.

Boats gather in the Inner Harbor for the annual "Swiftsure Classic",
an international race sponsored by the Pacific International Yachting
Association. This 37 year old race provides 136 miles of challenging sailing
from Victoria to the west coast of the Island and back.

Tours on land and water are available on the Yukon Queen, a vintage
sternwheeler, and bright red double-decker buses imported from England.

Ducks and swans frolic in a park-rimmed
fountain pool and the world's tallest
totem rises high above the treetops.
This gnarled oak is part of the largest
grove of oaks north of California.

The dome of Gonzales Dominion Observatory rises high on a bluff overlooking the Strait of Juan de Fuca. Visitors are always welcome and are sure to get an unobstructed view of the beautiful San Juan Islands and the snow-capped Olympics of Washington State.

A marine view near Ross Bay, where the fishing is good, the living easy and the sights supreme.

On the Scenic Drive, the Victoria Golf Club.

Snuggled into the next cove is Oak Bay Marina, offering facilities for yachtsmen and sports fishermen. A modern restaurant is located on the waterfront, just a few steps from the entrance to the Undersea Gardens.

A voyage to the bottom of the sea comes true at the Undersea Gardens. Hundreds of marine creatures in their natural habitat are seen through windows beneath sea level. Scuba divers hand feed the fish and pull shy octopuses from their murky dens and bring them in for a closer look.

There is vigorous development at the Gordon Head campus of the University of Victoria, as new buildings are raised to meet the increasing demands on this young unversity. At present, 5,500 students are enrolled in Arts and Science, Education, Fine Arts and Graduate Studies.

The spectacular site of the campus gives students an opportunity to see across Haro Strait and the San Juan Islands to Washington's 10,778 foot Mount Baker gleaming in the distance.

Fable Cottage, overlooking beautiful Cordova Bay, was built by Mr. and Mrs. B. Rogers. They have surrounded their unique storybook home with soft green lawns and flowers, preserving the natural growth of arbutus, dogwood and fir. The setting, the style, and the sweeping, graceful lines of Fable Cottage suggest fairyland, with a hint of brownies, gnomes and pixies lurking nearby. Barrel doors, knotted beams, hand-adzed furniture, old guns, a walk-through fireplace and many family heirlooms enchant visitors.

Spencer Castle is located on the highest point of land within Victoria city. It was built early in this century by architect Henry Sandham Griffith, and sold to David Spencer, department store magnate. The Spencer family spent over fifty years developing the famous rock gardens and gathering authentic elegant furnishings of the turn-of-the-century period. Spencer Castle is now open to the public and there is a spectacular 360 degree view from the four storey granite turret, reminiscent of the battlements of Windsor Castle in England.

Rich oak panelling, crystal chandeliers and priceless candelabra give a glimpse of past splendor.

Beaver Lake Park and adjoining Elk Lake
are action stations for swimmers and
water skiers. Tranquil picnic spots around
both lakes provide shady and restful
settings for pleasant outings.

This bookish barrier is the entrance to an
enchanted forest fairyland.

More than sixty favorite childhood friends peep out of their woodland glades.
Humpty Dumpty is on the verge of his fall; Jack and Jill appear with crowns still intact;
Peter Pumpkin Eater disciplines his wife and Hansel and Gretel stand transfixed
before the tempting gingerbread house of the wicked witch.

The Dominion Astrophysical Observatory on West Saanich Road
houses a 72 inch telescope, one of the largest in Canada.
A second and smaller 'scope sweeps the heavens from the new
dome. All coastal seismographic surveys are conducted here and
the facilities are used by students and researchers. Public
viewing hours enable visitors to marvel at the Pacific
region skies by night.

BUTCHART GARDENS

Butchart Gardens at Tod Inlet, 13 miles from Victoria is the outstanding showplace of the Pacific Northwest.

The Gardens began as a hobby in 1904 when Mr. and Mrs. Robert Pim Butchart slowly started changing the bleakness of an abandoned limestone quarry into a 25-acre wonderland. The gardens are still being expanded today by Ian Ross, grandson of the founders.

Through skilfull blending of trees, plants and exotic shrubs – many collected personally on their extensive world travels – the Butcharts created their own living memorial.

The Sunken Garden is a panorama of breathtaking color 50 feet below the entrance level. Here two fine arbor-vitae stand tall and proud with dense foliage in their natural symmetry. The once bleak sides of the exhausted quarry now hang with luxuriant green ivy and virginia creeper. The floor is a riot of color with roses, gentians, candytuft and so many species of rock and alpine flower that listing them is nearly impossible. They are planted right to the base of the towering walls. One of the many paths leads to an artificial lake that fills up a deep quarry pit and to a waterfall cascading down the steep bank.

Views from the Rose Garden, at its peak in color and variety in early July.

Water lilies grow in profusion in the Sunken Garden pools.

In the Italian Garden, a Renaissance lily pond is fed by a mermaid and fish fountain, bordered with flower beds.

Japanese Garden.

Cascading water in the Ross
Fountain reaches a peak of
70 feet, providing a
magnificent display by day
and an even more
spectacular view at night
when illuminated.

Trappers and pioneers of Vancouver Island built the original Fort Victoria, destroyed long ago by the march of metropolitanism. This replica of the old fort bastion serves as a museum, housing relics of the past.

Craigflower Manor House on Portage Inlet is another historic site in Victoria, built in 1853 by Kenneth Mackenzie, bailiff of the Puget Sound Agricultural Company. Today a museum, it was once the leading mansion in the young colony of Vancouver Island. The heavy entrance door is studded with hand forged nails and swings on massive wrought iron hinges to guard the precious furnishings that came around the Horn on the Mackenzies' voyage from Scotland over one hundred years ago.

The old Craigflower
Schoolhouse, built in 1855,
displays the Craigflower
farm implements of
a century ago,
the pioneer school room
and the original school bell.

The Rocky Point Stagecoach,
once fashionable mode
of transport, rests at the
Craigflower Schoolhouse Museum.

A stroll down Chaucer Lane
in the English Village
leads to Anne Hathaway's
cottage and a replica of
William Shakespeare's birthplace.

Fort Rodd Hill is a coastal artillery installation started in 1895 as part of the coastal defense system designed to protect Esquimalt Harbour and the growing commercial facilities of Victoria Harbour. With the approach of World War II, updated defenses were installed to replace the 19th century 6-inch BL guns, and the 12-pounder QF guns.

In 1962 the Fort Rodd Hill property was declared a National Historic Park and is still undergoing a continuing development plan. The restoration will include Fisgard Lighthouse, now joined to the foreshore of Fort Rodd Hill by a causeway. The Fisgard light has been warning and guiding ships since 1860, and stands 47 feet above its 13-foot wide granite base. It is built of brick brought around the Horn from England.

Hatley Castle was built on the 650-acre Hatley Park Estate by the Honourable James Dunsmuir. His father, Robert Dunsmuir, developed the rich coal veins at Nanaimo and Comox and built the well known Craigdarroch Castle in Victoria.

The lavish castle was planned by Samuel McLure and built of local stone, trimmed with Valdez and Saturna Island sandstone. Inside, oak and rosewood paneled the rooms, teak was used for flooring and local stone for the estate wall cost $75,000.00 in the year 1908.
The 82 foot high turret overlooks the impressive grounds, which, in the days of the Dunsmuirs, were maintained by one hundred men.

Besides his contribution to early British Columbia, and leaving this imposing landmark, the Honourable James Dunsmuir served his province well as Premier from 1900-1902, and as Lieutenant Governor from 1906 to 1909.

In 1940, Hatley Castle became a naval training establishment, H.M.C.S. Royal Roads. Now it is a Tri-Service Cadet College where cadets undergo two-year academic courses. The castle is the administrative building and other estate buildings have been converted to specialized uses.

The grounds still retain much of the original charm planned by
Messrs. Hall & Bett, Landscape artists of Boston, Massachusetts, who designed
the gardens and surroundings for the Dunsmuir family.

Frontier Village, nestled
in two and one half
acres of evergreens,
is a reconstructed ghost
town with the authentic
atmosphere of pioneer
days in early B.C.
This museum village
delights visitors with
a display of artifacts
of the horse drawn era
and many unique samples
of B.C. Indian
arts and crafts.

The Malahat Drive, part of
the Trans-Canada Highway,
follows the eastern coast
of the Island on its way
north of Victoria through
Duncan and Nanaimo.
Like most others on the
Island, this highway has an
excellent surface for
pleasurable driving and
offers spectacular views
of the Gulf of Georgia
and its myriad islands.

This covered wagon,
situated beside the
highway, is a relic of
earlier and slower days of
transportation.

DUNCAN

Duncan and the Cowichan Valley lie 38 miles north of Victoria on the Trans Canada Highway. This is a 600 square mile coastal plain with a serene rural character bolstered by convenient transportation to the capital city on the south and bustling Nanaimo to the north.

Lumbering, sawmills, pulp manufacturing and specialized farming support the growing population of the Valley and choice residential areas are home to 25,000 people. The flowering dogwood tree, B.C.'s floral emblem, grows in abundance and holly from the Valley brightens the Christmas holiday for people all over the world. Cowichan Indian Sweaters, knitted by local native women, are eagerly sought by sportsmen.

Recreational advantages are found at every twist and turn of the highway or the excellent secondary roads which criss-cross the area. Salmon fishing is enjoyed all along the Cowichan coast and Cowichan Bay, five miles below Duncan, is a mecca for resident and visiting fishermen who try for spring, coho, bluebacks or grilse in the summer and fall. Steelhead sea trout come into the streams from November to March and cutthroat and brown trout are also favorite catches.

One mile north of Duncan is the Cowichan Valley Forest Museum.

Cowichan Lake is 21 miles long and varies from one to one and one half miles wide. At its deepest point it measures 632 feet. The lake is situated in the famous Cowichan timber country and supports three giant mills which process and ship B.C. lumber all over the world.

The tranquil waters in
Cowichan Bay shelter
pleasure craft, fishing
boats and tugs, work
horses of the sea.
Readings taken over a
period of years shows an
annual average
temperature of 50 degrees.

Petroglyph Park, just south of Nanaimo, is an archaeological riddle of indeterminate age. The carvings, first seen by white men in 1860, are totally different from Indian art. The Indians themselves claim the petroglyphs were done by a race that inhabited this area long before they came. Scientists agree, and estimate the carvings to be 15,000 years old.

Another evidence of the culture of this early race is the Hepburn Stone, found near the Nanaimo River on the site of a well excavation in 1923. This stone, with carved human features and an oriental-like headdress, is preserved in the Nanaimo Bastion.

NANAIMO

Among the sentinel firs and sheltering cedars on Vancouver Island at Wintuhysen Bay, so named by one of the first Spanish navigators, lived five bands of Indians who stayed together under a loose sort of confederacy which they called "Sne-ny-mo", meaning 'the whole' or 'big strong tribe.'

The western world was already encroaching upon the natural wonders of the Island. The Hudsons Bay men from Fort Victoria, built in 1843, were venturing further afield in this Island paradise.

In 1849 a chief among the Sne-ny-mo tribes found some black rock while clam digging. He threw it on the camp fire and found that it burned. Almost a year later this Indian chief visited the Hudson's Bay Company fort to have his gun fixed by a blacksmith, and saw this same black 'rock' burning in the forge. He remarked that there was plenty of the black rock where he lived. For a small reward he promised to bring a sample. The coal was tested and found to be of excellent quality, so HBC factor James Douglas dispatched Joseph W. McKay to the Inlet commonly called 'Nanymo Bay' to formally take possession of the coal beds. This was the year 1852.

Mining operations began and in 1853 the Hudson's Bay Company started a settlement overlooking the water. One of the original buildings stands today – the Bastion – a famed and cherished landmark, the pride of Nanaimo's people and a historic site for tourists.

The town was first called Colviletown, after Andrew Colvile, then Governor of the Hudson's Bay Company, but in 1860 this name gave way to the familiar Nanaimo, so spelled by Joseph McKay in a letter dated by him in March, 1853, and obviously an anglicized spelling of the Indian "Sne-ny-mo".

As years passed and the mining continued successfully, Nanaimo grew and prospered and the city was incorporated in 1874 with a population of approximately 1,500. Tramp steamers flying flags from all ports of the world bunkered at this Island port to load the precious coal from these deposits, the largest on the Pacific Coast.

In and around the growing city new developments were started. Rich farming soil was opened up, fishing and lumbering forged ahead and Nanaimo's strategic shipping position was becoming firmly established. When the demand for coal ceased, the city made a transition into other industries and services quite easily.

Today, Nanaimo is home to nearly 16,000 people with 35,000 counted in Greater Nanaimo. Deepsea fishing vessels arrive laden with salmon, cod and herring and at neighboring Departure Bay stands the modern building and laboratories of the Pacific Biological Station of the Fisheries Research Board of Canada. Farming produces sheep, poultry, and eggs, dairy goods, small fruits and vegetables. Lumbering and lumber by-products have become major industries with over one thousand people employed in pulp production alone.

Nanaimo provides ample deepsea ship anchorage in her sheltered harbor. It is the northernmost point of a protected waterway extending from Puget Sound in Washington on up through the beautiful Gulf Islands. It is the main point of entry and export for the Island as well as a major communications centre for travel between the Island and mainland.

HERITAGE – preserved in an Indian longboat and in the Bastion of the original Hudson's Bay settlement.

WOOD – vast forests provide the raw material for modern mills.

COAL – first important product of Nanaimo is given a Centennial homage in this monument fittingly poised on a base of real coal.

Berthed in Nanaimo, a replica of the Beaver, first steam driven
paddle wheeler to sail North Pacific waters.

Leafy glades and a murmuring millstream bid welcome
to Bowen Park, an emerald refuge in the heart of the city.

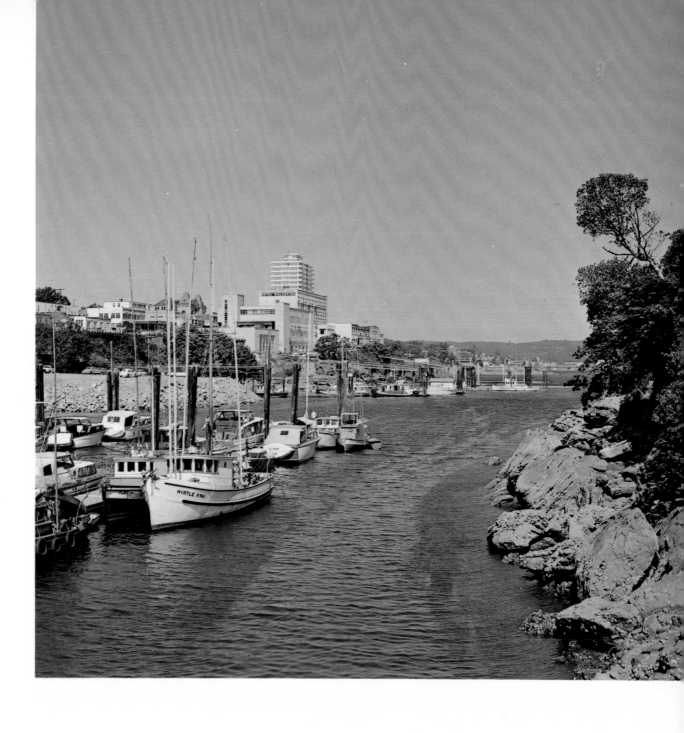

Fishing boats and pleasure craft tie up in the very shadow of modern development.
The water route is one of the important spokes leading to the Hub City of Nanaimo.

A telephoto shot from near Parksville on the highway leading to the Alberni Valley, shows 5,962 foot Mount Arrowsmith dominating the skyline, just as it towers over the twin pulp cities of Alberni and Port Alberni in the valley. The highway from Parksville junction to the Albernis leads through some of the most magnificent scenery on the Island and is a virtual holiday paradise for hikers, anglers, hunters and camera fans.

In Little Qualicum Falls
Provincial Park, pine sweet
air and cool green glades
encourage strolling along
the well kept paths.

The sparkling waters of
Cameron Lake refresh the
eye weary of highway grey.

From Parksville to the Alberni Valley,
Highway #4 winds through
MacMillan Park. This 31-mile stretch
of virgin timber is also known as
Cathedral Grove. Centuries old
Douglas fir stand like lofty pillars
to support their green transluscent
dome of boughs high above.

Winding paths lead into the dewy
depths where creatures of the forest
enjoy peace and protection, and
spiders spin their delicate webs to
be caressed only by morning sun
and evening breezes.

Leaving the twin cities of Alberni and Port Alberni behind, the Tofino Highway twists onward and passes beautiful Sproat Lake.

The rugged mountain
road leads through the
MacKenzie Range,
last barrier to
the broad sweep of
the Pacific.

First settlement facing the Pacific is Ucluelet, tucked away in a pretty cove at the seaward end of Barkley Sound. This is a safe refuge for the large fleet of salmon trollers that reap the silver harvest on the wide Pacific beyond the light.

The sea spills out her wealth of specimens at Amphitrite Point. Clefts carved by the waves and shallow tidal pools give up their treasures easily to a sure footed collector.

Brilliant rock flowers tempt the naturalist and bloom in colorful contrast to the barren rock and broiling sea.

The unfettered force of the great water body breaks finally in these immense rollers on the white sands of Long Beach, carrying odd mementos from Japan.

Rain, wind and sun bleached the barren limbs of this once mighty
giant of the forest. The same elements nurture the tender shoots
of new growth, completing nature's never-ending cycle.

The West Coast rain
forest protects the
delicate growth of
deer fern and exquisite
wild flowers.

Massive boulders at
Wreck Bay brace
themselves for the
onslaught of the
incoming tide.

Pacific oysters, another of the rich
delicacies of the sea, are harvested at
Fanny Bay, north of Qualicum
Beach. Ten miles of leased oyster
beds lie along the shore, and though the
public is allowed on the beach
to watch the interesting shucking
operations, no oysters may be taken
from this area. In spring, fall and
winter oyster harvesters are in full
swing gathering this gourmet's
delight to be speeded fresh daily
to markets and restaurants
across the nation.

Still further north on the Coastal Highway, is the Comox Valley, with the centres of Courtenay and Comox. This pleasant agricultural valley offers many attractions to the visitor who wishes to golf, fish, hike, climb mountains, ski at the well-groomed slopes of Forbidden Plateau, or participate in water sports.

A marina in the heart of Courtenay.

Miracle Beach Park is one mile off the main highway between Courtenay and Campbell River, heavily forested with Douglas fir, hemlock and broadleaf maple. Between this evergreen wall and the smooth sandy beaches are modern accommodations awaiting holidayers – especially the fisherman.

At low tide, abundant sea life delights children and craggy stumps assume shapes to suit their imaginative games.

CAMPBELL RIVER

Fishing boats over the Tyee Hole.

A regular visitor to Campbell River once said, "You can spend five years hunting, fishing and hiking around this area and you still won't have seen all of it."

Campbell River offers a vast scenic area where relaxation and outdoor recreation are found in abundance by fast flowing streams, placid lakes, and the restless sea that boils through Seymour Narrows in Discovery Passage.

This is the rich industrial area of northern Vancouver Island where modern logging operations and the large newsprint mills provide interesting sights, and the dam and powerhouse supply most of the power for the Island.

The name Campbell River is synonymous with the Tyee, mighty fighting fish of the Pacific. This is home base for the world famous Tyee Club of British Columbia, Canada's leading competitive sport fishing organization. Catching a salmon over 30 pounds on regulation tackle qualifies a new member.

The dignity of native culture is evident in this outstanding example of Indian Art.

Fishing boats at anchor in Campbell River Harbour.

CAMPBELL RIVER FIRE

On a hot day in July 1938, an ominous smoke pillar near Gosling Lake signalled a forest fire which was to ravage 115 square miles of logged and timbered land. Over 1500 firefighters battled grimly for weeks to save timber and communities. Costs and damages were enormous. Reforestation, intensified by the Forest Service, helped to heal the black scar.

PROVINCE OF BRITISH COLUMBIA

A bleak reminder of the time it takes nature to heal carelessly inflicted wounds. In 1938 the great Campbell River Fire burned for weeks as 115 square miles of logged and timbered land was laid waste. Slowly the scars heal, but a scant 30 years later the devastation is still evident. Logging goes on, however, and dust rising behind a lumber carrier is a reminder that timber-dry forests blaze quickly from a hastily thrown match or embers left by campers.

The cascading beauty of the waters in Elk Falls Park provides contrast to the desolation of fire ravaged timber lands.

Giant diesel trucks carry their heavy cargo to the mills from the vast logging operations of Crown Zellerbach.

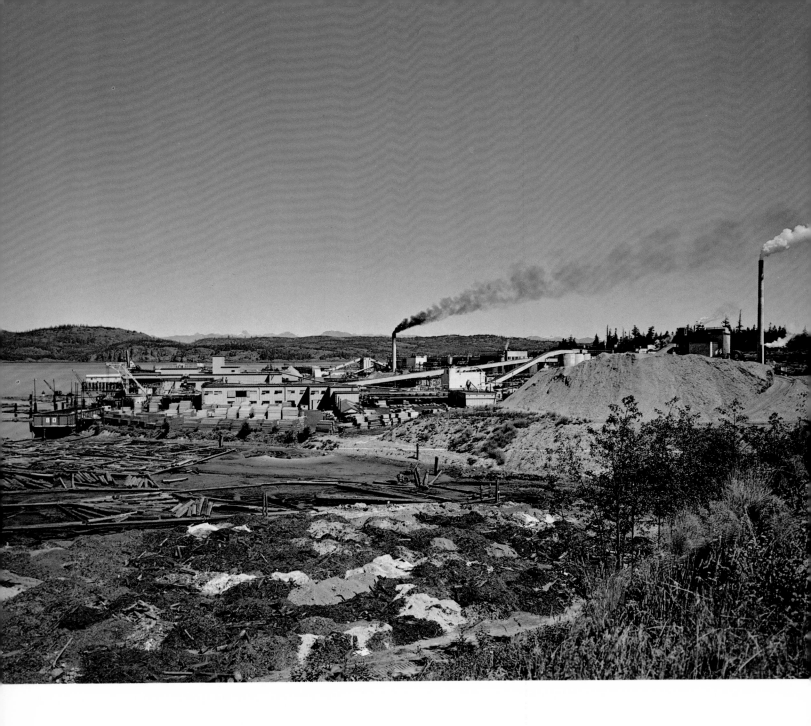

An important contribution to the industrial wealth of this area – the Crown Zellerbach
Elk Falls Division Pulp and Paper Mill and Sawmill, producing lumber, bleached and unbleached
kraft pulp and paper, and newsprint for markets across the nation and around the world.

Treacherous currents and swirling eddies in Seymour Narrows still harass vessels despite the 1958 blasting of Ripple Rock, twin underwater peaks which claimed numerous ships and lives.

A view beside Roberts Lake on the highway to Kelsey Bay.

The Sayward Valley hugs the banks of the Salmon River and is hemmed in by mountains. This strangely beautiful part of northern Vancouver Island is a scarcely populated land where logging is a way of life and commercial and sports fishermen seek the bounty of sea and stream.

Highway 19 from Campbell River to Kelsey Bay is a vital link in the B.C. Highways and ferries system. About three hours of smooth, rapid road travel from Nanaimo, through Campbell River and the Sayward Valley, brings you to Kelsey Bay where you can board the vessel Queen of Prince Rupert for the spectacular Inside Passage route to Prince Rupert. From there the traveler may continue north to Alaska or east through the interior of British Columbia.

A fitting climax to a pleasant holiday on Vancouver Island . . . a British Columbia sunset
and the brilliant silhouette of the Canadian flag flying proudly from the stern of a B.C. Ferries vessel.

**The world is a great book,
of which they who never stir
from home read only a page.**

St. Augustine

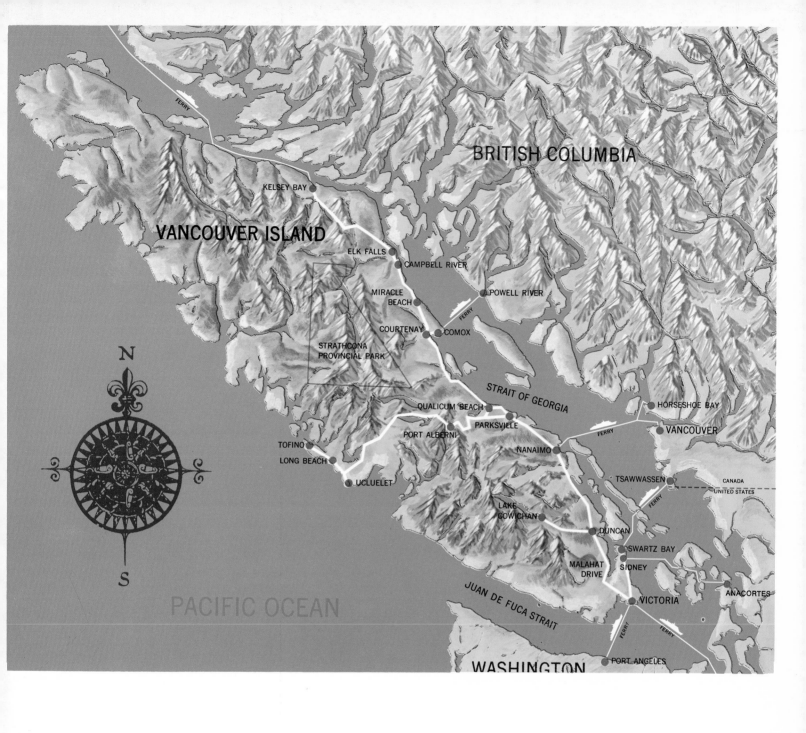

CREDITS
Published by:
Spectrum Enterprises Ltd.
910 Beach Avenue
Vancouver 1, B.C.
Canada

Colour reproduction by:
Coast Colour Reproductions Ltd.
Vancouver, B.C., Canada

Photographs courtesy of B.C. Government:
Page 5 – B.C. Government Ferries
Page 9 – B.C. Legislative Assembly Chamber
Page 14 – Swiftsure Boats
Page 43 – Cowichan Valley Forest Museum
Page 60 – Aerial view of Long Beach
Page 70 – Tyee Club – Fishing at Tyee Pool